Centred on Christ

CWR

Michael Baughen

Published 2013 by CWR, Waverley Abbey House, Waverley Lane, Farnham, Surrey GU9 8EP, UK.
Registered Charity No. 294387. Registered Limited Company No. 1990308.

For list of National Distributors visit www.cwr.org.uk/distributors

Concept development, editing, design and production by CWR

Cover images: istock and fotosearch

Printed in the UK by Stephens and George

ISBN: 978-1-78259-017-0

Contents

Introduction

It is a joy for me to have the privilege of writing this Lent Study Guide for you. The letter to the Philippians has been such a blessing to me in my life and I hope I can enrich your own blessing from it through these studies.

My actual introduction to the theme of the letter is in Study One, as I want everyone to read it and introductions often get skipped!

However, I hope all participants will take time to read Acts 16:16–40 to get the background. This was Paul's first stop in his call to Europe and characters like Lydia and the jailor and the girl possessed by an evil spirit all spring vividly to our minds. So does the dramatic incident of Paul and Silas, with feet fastened in the stocks, praying and singing hymns at midnight. They certainly rejoiced in the Lord and not in circumstances (Phil. 4:4)! So the gospel came memorably to Philippi and a church was born; the church now receiving this letter.

One other suggestion: we are looking at our Lord through the vehicle of a Pauline letter. *Please* would you try to set aside time during Lent to read the whole of a Gospel, straight through in one day, or over two or three days. Better still, read all four Gospels. Then our studies will link into your seeing our Lord afresh, through that Gospel, in His grace, humility, servanthood, authority and self-sacrifice.

May you know Christ more and draw closer to Him during this Lent season.

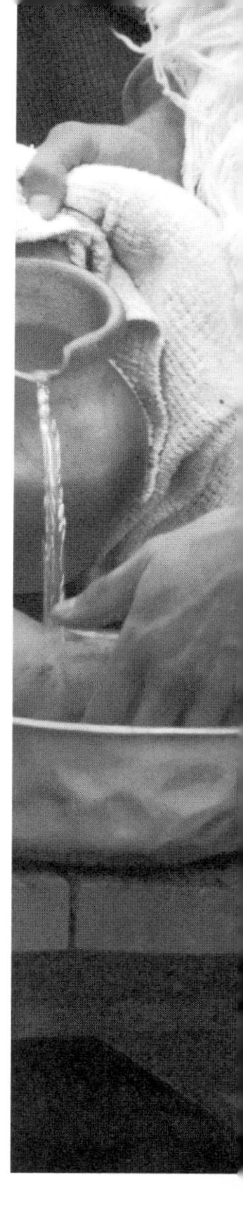

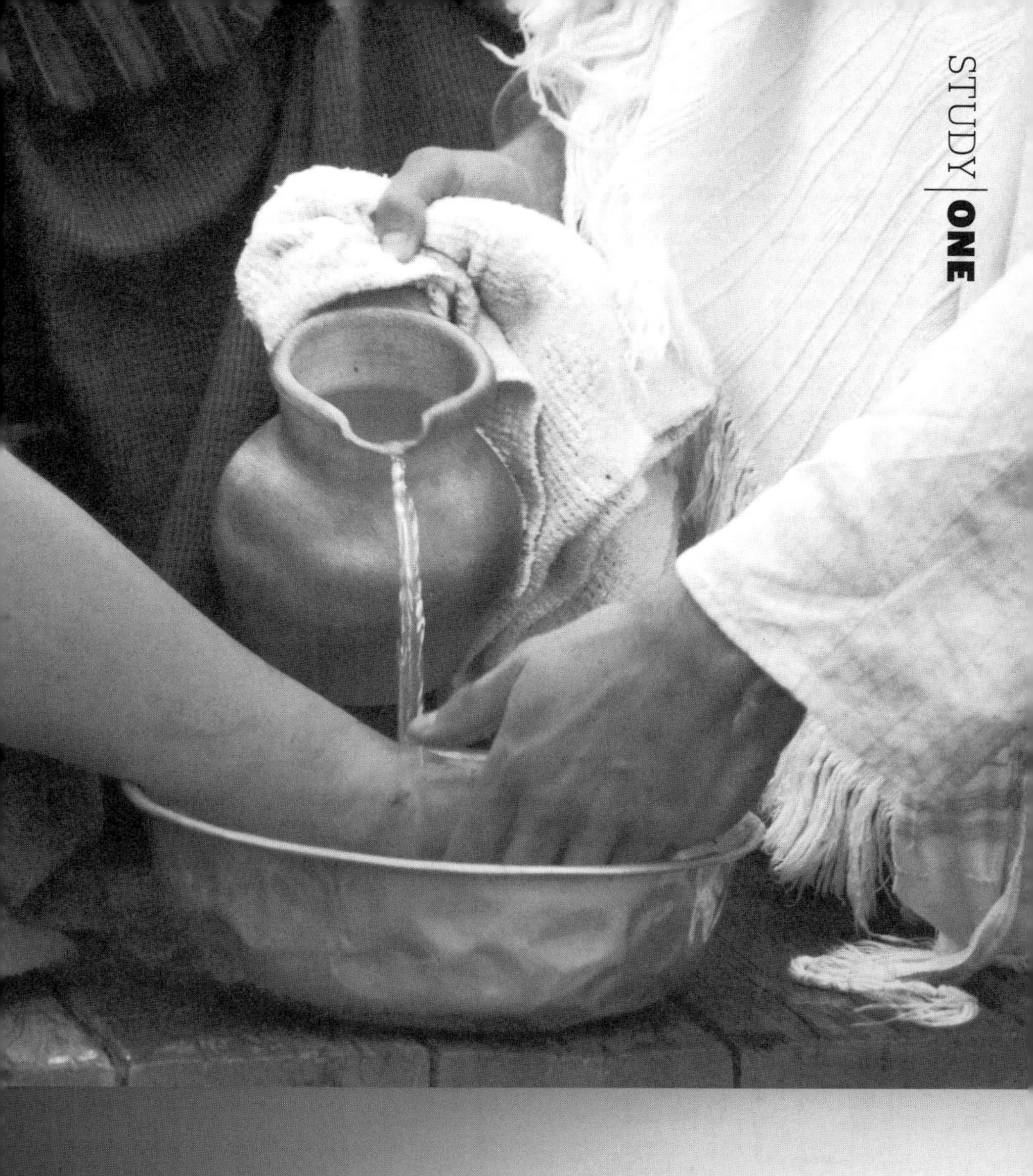

STUDY | ONE

Servants of Christ

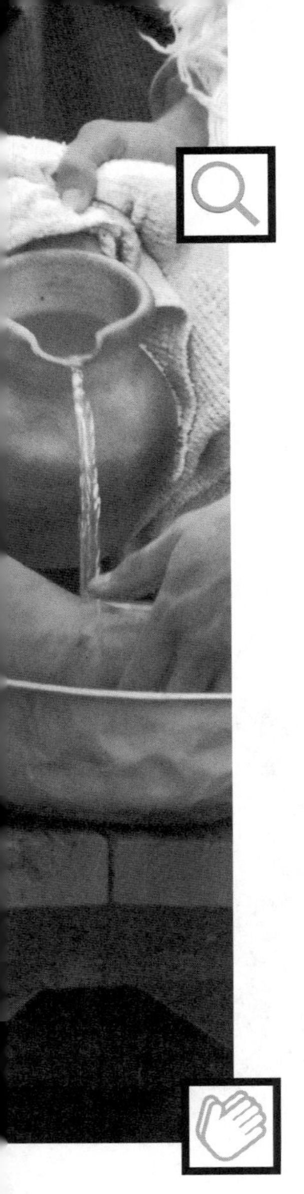

Focusing

Choose some object in the room where you are sitting and imagine you are taking a quick snap with your mobile phone. Look at it for five seconds, then turn away and think about what you have seen. Look again, this time imagining you have a high-quality camera aiming to produce a quality photo ... positioning, light, focus. Look at the object for, say, fifteen seconds, then look away and think how much more you have taken in about the object. Finally, look at it again, this time imagining you are going to paint the scene ... now take a minute or so ... look, yes, at angle, light and focus. But now you will have to gaze into it more deeply, discerning colour differences and subtleties, shadows, perspective and how you can make the picture of a place or person live, getting under the surface of your subject.

All our studies are from Paul's letter to the Philippians. So often we come to Scripture and read in smallish chunks. It is, as it were, a snapshot approach. If we do that we will usually say this letter is about rejoicing or rejoicing in Christ; if we come like a camera and try to see the whole letter it will dawn on us that Christ is mentioned in more than half the verses and so will no doubt resolve it is about Christ our Lord.

But coming to it like a painter we will look more deeply, observing shades and textures, sensing more deeply what is being conveyed. When we do that we will, I suggest, see that the whole letter reaches into the depths of the *humility and servanthood* of Christ and our need to be like that ourselves.

Opening Prayer

Gracious Lord, as we come to this study of Your Word, we pray that You will give us the eyes to see You more clearly, to see more deeply into this part of Your Word than we have ever done before, and to be deeply changed in our lives with You and for You. Amen.

Bible Reading

Philippians 1:1–2

[1]'Paul and Timothy, servants of Christ Jesus, To all the saints in Christ Jesus at Philippi, together with the overseers and deacons. [2]Grace and peace to you from God our Father and the Lord Jesus Christ.'

Reflection

A snapshot of these opening verses would just see a greeting, but if you look closely there is more being expressed here. Paul starts most of his letters as an apostle – for example, his letter to the Ephesians begins 'Paul, an apostle' and in his letter to the Colossians he adds 'and Timothy our brother', but not here. Timothy is associated on equal terms in the greeting. Both are servants of Christ. 'Apostle' is not used. Why?

Look on to chapter 2:3–4 and you will see that the Philippians had trouble with self-interest: 'Do nothing out of selfish ambition or vain conceit, but in humility consider others better than yourselves. Each of you should look not only to your own interests, but to the interests of others.' Later on in chapter 4:2 we read: 'I plead with Euodia and I plead with Syntyche to agree with each other in the Lord.' Were they disputing about who was better at mission or who was the leader or who should have priority of place? We do not know, but whatever it was, it was harming the gospel witness.

Paul thus deliberately starts the letter as he means to go on, pressing the need for humility as God's servants. He sets aside his God-given role as an apostle and instead starts with declaring his oneness in servanthood with Timothy.

One evening when I was at All Souls, Langham Place we had the *St Paul Oratorio* sung, in the middle of which I preached a short sermon on Paul as a servant of Christ. Immediately as I reached the door at the end of the service, a man bore down on me. He took me by the lapels and shouted, 'I am not a servant of Christ ... I am a child of God, freed by His precious blood'. Before he fled into Regent Street, I took

him by the lapels and said, 'So am I ... but if you know the letter to the Romans you will know that after the magnificent chapters on sin, the cross and new life in the Spirit we have chapter 12 where we are urged, (verse 1) because of God's mercy, to offer ourselves as living sacrifices. Servanthood is not forced on us; it is a voluntary response. It is deliberately taking up the towel to serve wherever or however God wants. That may be in a leading position or quietly in the background, but it is willing, sacrificial service and not status seeking.'

We will see how this teaching works through this letter, but now look on to the second half of chapter two. Throughout my ministry I have frequently said to myself and to others when an idea is introduced, 'Earth it'. Paul 'earths' this teaching on humility and servanthood first with our Lord (2:7 '… taking the very nature of a servant…') which we will look at in a later study, but then in the second half of chapter two with people – people his readers knew well. Imagine how they felt when these penetrating and powerful examples were spelt out to them.

Philippians 2:19–24 is about Timothy: in verse 20 Paul writes, 'I have no-one else like him, who takes a genuine interest in your welfare. For everyone looks out for his own interests, not those of Jesus Christ' which would immediately bring to mind the many ways Timothy had served so well. Verses 25–30 are about Epaphroditus, '... he almost died for the work of Christ, risking his life to make up for the help you could not give me' (v30). Here was a man of great love and action, and remarkable self-sacrifice. What Paul writes about these two is very moving.

This humility of servanthood was a hard lesson for the disciples to learn and they were slow in doing so. In Mark 10 we see James and John asking (v37) 'Let one of us sit at your right and the other at your left in your glory'. Breathtaking isn't it? But oh so human! The ten are indignant, possibly because they didn't get in first? Jesus presses home the exact opposite as the manner of life He expects from His followers, '... whoever wants to become great among you must be your servant, and whoever wants to be first must be slave of all' (v43). Wow!

Then the punch line, 'For even the Son of Man did not come to be served, but to serve, and to give his life as a ransom for many' (v45).

When they still could not take it in, He stunned them in the days before the crucifixion when He took the towelling of a servant and washed His disciples' feet (John 13). As you will probably know, Peter reacted. But let us remind ourselves of what our Lord said after He had finished, 'Do you understand what I have done for you? ... You call me "Teacher" and "Lord", and rightly so, for that is what I am. Now that I, your Lord and Teacher, have washed your feet, you also should wash one another's feet. I have set you an example that you should do as I have done for you ... Now that you know these things, you will be blessed if you do them' (v12–15,17). A never-to-be-forgotten lesson; not that we should literally wash feet (except symbolically) but that we should be servants to one another and not be status-conscious.

How often must our Lord have sought to bring about this revolutionary change of attitude; this over-turning of the world's attitudes about greatness and the change to His radical new way of thinking, to this counter-culture? We have to put up with endless plaudits for so-called stars these days, but in God's book the plaudits will be much more for the humble servant, often serving others quietly but persistently, ready for self-sacrifice if necessary.

Yes, we have titles and leadership positions, but unless these are held in a spirit of humble service they are empty titles.

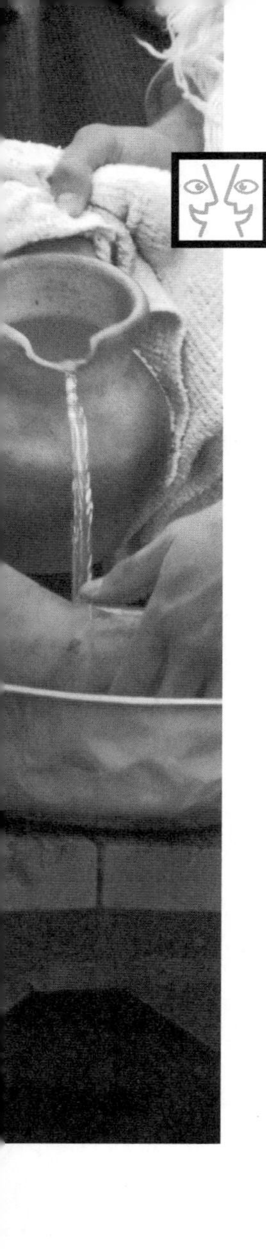

Discussion Starters

1. I was very apprehensive of the trappings that would surround me as a Bishop and so I resolved to put a piece of towelling in my cassock pocket so that every time I reached for a handkerchief, I would touch the towelling and be reminded I was to be servant of all. I fear I still often failed my Lord in this, but the towelling helped a lot. Will you share within the group what has challenged you or helped you on this issue, for example, times when you were brought up short on this or suddenly saw yourself as others see you? Are there other thoughts about how to remind yourself to walk in the humility of Christ as a servant?

2. How far can we be affected/infected by the spirit of the age ... keeping up with the Jones's, the latest fashion, the most money, striving for more authority (in church life or the rest of life), ie the standards of the world, not the way of Christ the servant?

3. In what ways has the church been a servant community to the world in history?

4. What marks out your home church as a servant community? Could it be more so?

5. Is there a danger that if we major on service we may get slack about our walk with Christ, with our daily times of meditating on His Word, with real prayer or worship, or of growing in our knowledge of the faith? If so, how do we keep a balanced Christian life?

6. Who has most inspired you as a true servant of Christ, either in history or as a contemporary? Share within the group, discerning what it is that makes them so truly a servant of Christ.

Worship

Say or sing together *Purify my heart* (Brian Doerksen) or a similar song.

Final Thoughts

I can think of hundreds of examples of those calling themselves Christians who have denied their profession by their lifestyle, their pride, their self-centredness, their abuse of authority and so on, *but* we can make ourselves feel comfortable by doing that, persuading ourselves that we are not like them.

So let us now ask ourselves some questions:

1. Jesus said (Luke 16:13), 'You cannot *serve* [my emphasis] both God and Money'.

Is that issue sorted and checked in our lives?

2. In Matthew 25:14–30 Jesus taught the parable of the talents. One servant was given five talents, the next was given two, and the final servant was given one. All were to use their talents as the stewards of the Master. The first two brought a 100% return, the first bringing another five talents and the second bringing another two. Both are commended with the words, 'Well done, good and faithful servant'. It is noteworthy that it is their faithfulness that is re-emphasised in what follows. It is the laziness of the third servant that brings condemnation.

Sometimes people have said to me, 'I have no talents to use' (Eph. 4:7 says the opposite). That is pathetic. Everybody has talents. So even though we may not be ten-talents people we can serve faithfully even with one. So how faithful are we with our God-given talent(s)? If we are uncertain how to serve, let us ask our Lord, with an open mind as the answer may be unexpected, surprising, even life-changing!

3. If, because of age or because of physical problems, we cannot serve our Lord as we used to, can we/will we still seek to serve Him in some other ways? My mother-in-law was

someone who served others through her life as a Christian but in her late nineties, totally blind and without ability left to switch on talking books and so on, she happily served her Lord by praying for everyone she could think of, working through the alphabet with names starting with A, then B and through to Z (yes, one great-grandchild was a Z!) Faithful indeed! Is that an encouragement to us?

So this first study will only be effective if we now use a time of silence in the group or when we get home, and deliberately talk to our Lord, laying our life before Him, asking Him to show us where we are infected by the world and where or how we might better be His servants in lifestyle, in action and in witness – the results of such prayer and meditation could be surprising.

Meditation

My suggestion is that there is now five minutes of quiet for personal meditation.

Worship

It would seem appropriate to sing or say together Graham Kendrick's song *From Heaven You Came*, also known as *The Servant King*.

Closing Prayer

Teach us, good Lord,
To serve You as You deserve;
To give and not to count the cost,
To fight and not to heed the wounds,
To labour and not to seek for any reward save that of knowing that we do Your will,
Through Jesus Christ our Lord. Amen.

Prayer of St Ignatius Loyola, slightly modernised.

STUDY | **TWO**

Affection of Christ

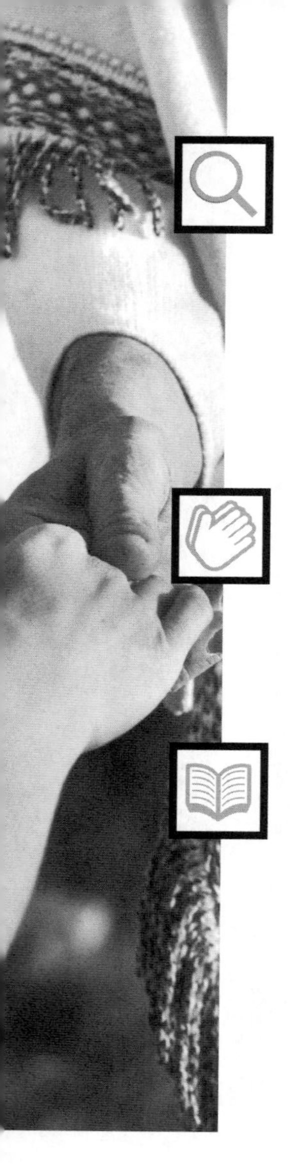

Focusing

Think of a favourite tree (perhaps a cherry tree in full blossom or an apple tree loaded with apples) depending on its roots. If there is a long drought then trees can wither as the root withers. As we come to Philippians 1:3–14, there are several attractive fruits to look at; gospel partnership, assurance and prayer are some of them. But they all spring from the root. After we have prayed, we will look at part one of our reading. As it is read, see the fruit – discern the root.

Opening Prayer

Dear Father, we come together to study Your Word. Please allow us to see beyond what we already know about this passage and to be open to how the Holy Spirit wants to apply it to us so that we may apply it in our lives. For the sake of Jesus Christ our Lord. Amen.

Bible Reading 1

Philippians 1:3-8

[3]'I thank my God every time I remember you. [4]In all my prayers for all of you, I always pray with joy [5]because of your partnership in the gospel from the first day until now, [6]being confident of this, that he who began a good work in you will carry it on to completion until the day of Christ Jesus.

[7]It is right for me to feel this way about all of you, since I have you in my heart; for whether I am in chains or defending and confirming the gospel, all of you share in God's grace with me. [8]God can testify how I long for all of you with the affection of Christ Jesus.'

Reflection

I am sure you will have seen that the root of this passage is Paul's 'having them in his heart' with 'the affection of Christ Jesus'. It is a deep root. *Affection* is a mild translation. The word Paul used means the chief intestines, the entrails, the bowels! This was regarded as the seat of emotions. Paul is conveying to them that his love for them is rooted deep down in his inner being and that his heart pounds and beats with the deep, self-giving, sacrificial, unconditional love of Christ. There is nothing superficial in such love. He 'longs' for them with this love (v8).

In most of his letters, Paul starts with praise or encouragement even though he may have criticism and correction to give further on. This letter is no exception. Most of us respond positively to encouragement and negatively to criticism. In my earlier days of trying to paint using watercolours, the teacher looked at my picture and said, 'That is entirely wrong, perspective hopeless, light and shadow wrong'. In a different group the teacher said to the student beginner, 'I admire your boldness, your use of colour, your free style(!), your personal expression'. Are we encouragers – a word, note, e-mail or phone call of appreciation, thanks or compliment; seeing the best and not the worst?

The first encouragement is that Paul prays for them. When he says 'every time I remember you' he does not mean the occasional prayer when he happens to remember them. His whole Rabbinic upbringing would have meant a regular organised rhythm of prayer, day by day. And it is 'for all of you' (v4) so both the good and the difficult are included. It is a privilege to know that a number of great Christians have truly prayed for one in detail until they went home to Christ. How much we owe them. Praying like this for a number of Christians, and telling them, can be a colossal encouragement to them as well as bringing blessing from the Lord in their Christian service and life. It is only when we love them with the affection of Christ that we will prioritise such prayer in our lives.

The second encouragement is expressing his joy because of their partnership in the gospel '... from the first day until now'

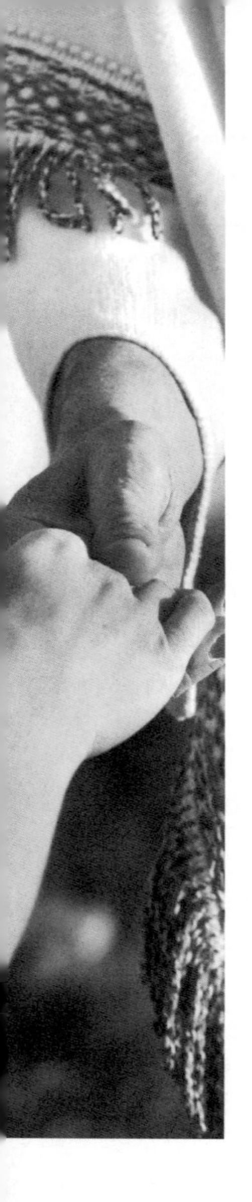

(v5). The 'now', of course, refers to his being in prison, when others might have given up witnessing. But not the Philippians. Christians on whom one can rely, who will always seek to do the best for Christ, who have the gospel of Christ burning in their heart, who will be practical in actions that advance the kingdom and express God's love in the world – they are worth their weight in gold. How sad for Paul when he wrote, in 2 Timothy 4:10, '… Demas, because he loved this world, has deserted me …' Later in Philippians, when we come to chapter 4, we will see how their support for Paul in practical ways never wavered. The sending of Epaphroditus (chapter 2) was part of that support. As one looks back over one's life, many wonderful servants of the gospel come to mind; but also the servants faithful in background support like the elderly lady who saw it as her Christian service to baby-sit for us every Friday evening in our curacy days while Myrtle and I ran the youth group. She was a vital part of God's blessing on that group.

The third encouragement is assurance. Such is the evidence of committed faith and service at Philippi that Paul lifts their eyes in the confidence of their work going on to completion until the Day of Christ. But in doing so he does not say *they* can do it but that *He* can do it. Early on in Christian service I sometimes wondered how I could keep going for another forty years. It was the encouragement and confidence of others that helped me to see that it was His work and His way; my part was to seek to know and do His will. In my eighties now, my testimony is, 'Yes, He can do it'.

The fourth encouragement is to Paul. There he is in prison and though, as we will see later in the letter, some took advantage of his situation, the Philippians remained faithful and so clearly shared 'in God's grace' with him (v7). Knowing God's amazing grace, rejoicing in that grace, living by that grace – all this unites us at the deepest level. As one gets to old age, it is one's great joy to see the grace of God at work in younger people and in the church.

So all of this springs from the root of love – the love that aches with Christ's love.

Discussion Starters

1. Share ways in which you have received encouragement from other Christians.

2. In what other ways do you think you could give encouragement to those younger in the faith and, perhaps, those getting older?

3. Discuss ways in which we can be 'partners in the gospel'.

4. How can we grow in having 'the affection of Christ' for our fellow-Christians?

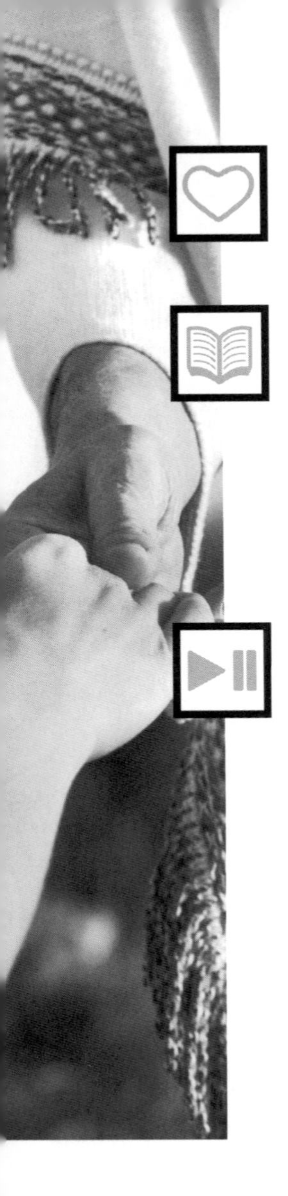

Worship

Sing or say the hymn *We have a gospel to proclaim* (Edward Burns) or *O Thou who camest from above* (Charles Wesley).

Bible Reading 2

Philippians 1:9–11

[9]'And this is my prayer: that your love may abound more and more in knowledge and depth of insight, [10]so that you may be able to discern what is best and may be pure and blameless until the day of Christ, [11]filled with the fruit of righteousness that comes through Jesus Christ – to the glory and praise of God.'

Reflection

Even non-Christians often say they pray for those they love (meaning their family), praying usually for their health, success or protection. Paul lifts us on to a totally different level as Christians. He **prays** for those for whom he has the affection of Christ (so a very wide embrace of people in Christ's family) and he does not pray for their health, success or preservation but for far higher things. He knows they love God and others but he **prays** that their love may 'abound' – this is an evocative word in the Greek which means to overflow, a superfluity, to become more prominent and even 'exuberance'. He longs for them to be truly and evidently a people of Christ's love. Yes, he has urged them and will do so again, to love one another, but he knows, as we should, that the work of the Spirit in hearts brings the warmth of that love, that God's love is '… poured out into our hearts by the Holy Spirit …' (Rom. 5:5). So he **prays** for that. He does so also in Ephesians 3:17–19, **praying** that they may be '… rooted and established in love …' (note the word 'root') and may '… grasp how wide and long and high and deep is the love of Christ …'

It was true in Paul's day and is even more so today, that the word 'love' can be so abused and loosely applied that morally wrong actions can be excused 'if there is love'. No, says Paul. So he **prays** that their love might abound 'more and more in *knowledge and depth of insight'* [my italics]. The 'knowledge' word is always about moral and spiritual knowledge. It is not banging on about some moral or spiritual issue as if you alone are right but it is getting inside the question, inside people, inside Scripture, inside situations.

The **prayer** goes on: '... so that you may be able to *discern* what is best ...' [my italics]. Some translate this as 'what is vital'. Other translations put it like this: '... enabling you to learn by experience what really matters ...' I find that helpful as I think of the many times when Christians have become almost militant about a very secondary aspect of belief or life rather than a primary one. It is so divisive, so unnecessary and so often tragic in its outcome. Presumably the divisions between Euodia and Syntyche in chapter 4 are of this nature, as Paul deems it possible that they could 'agree in the Lord' – in other words, in the centralities of the faith; in what is vital.

Pause to discuss the last three paragraphs.

(Reflection continued)

This **prayer** for love is also (v10) that they may be 'pure and blameless'. 'Pure' has the meaning of 'transparency' – what you see is what one is, rather than someone with a double life, or a hidden side. It also means 'unadulterated' and Paul's concern is that as they lived in a pagan city they could so easily not discern what is vital and what is not. This powerfully challenges us today in the materialistic and morally weakening society of which we are part. He then adds 'blameless', which means 'not causing harm to anyone' by our words or actions. 1 Corinthians 10:32 has the same word: 'Do not cause anyone to stumble ...' Hypocrisy, once exposed, can be terribly damaging to others. How we live can draw men to Christ or repel them. '... Let your light shine before men ...' (Matt. 5:16).

This is 'until the day of Christ ...' It is the whole of life, not giving up as we get older. Yet this is not a burden but a joy for it is so fulfilling to grow more like Christ in our daily living

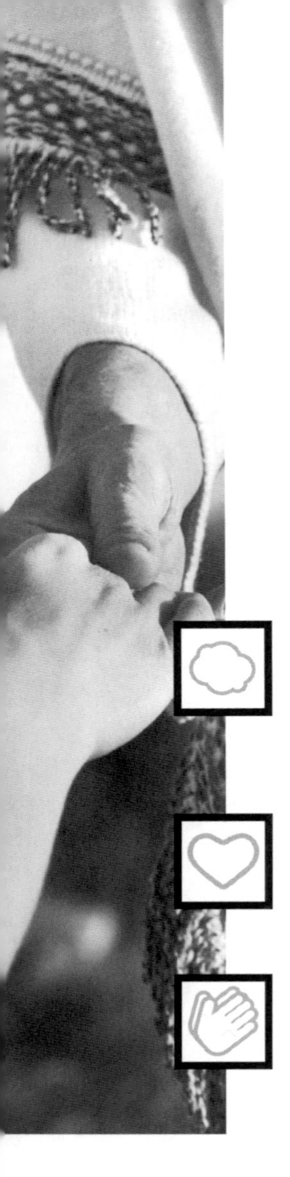

and to be a positive example to younger Christians. Living close to Christ, **praying** for this growth in love that discerns and blossoms, brings a harvest of 'righteousness that comes through Jesus Christ' and this brings glory and praise to God, not to us. This echoes our Lord's words, 'This is to my Father's glory, that you bear much fruit, showing yourselves to be my disciples' (John 15:8).

This great prayer flows out of the love of God; love is the root. It is a prayer that I hope you will write out and use every week for yourself and every member of the group meeting with you and for others in the church. Although prayer may cover physical or practical needs, it is spiritual growth in yourself and other Christians which is far, far more important and should always have priority.

Meditation

Share what has particularly struck you from this reflection on verses 9–11.

Spend a few minutes meditating personally on these verses.

Worship

Say or sing together Luke Connaugton's beautiful hymn *Love is his word, love is his way.*

Closing Prayer

(We pray Paul's prayer for ourselves and everyone else in the group.)

Gracious God, may our love abound more and more in knowledge and depth of insight, so that we may be able to discern what is best and may be pure and blameless until the day of Christ, filled with the fruits of righteousness that comes through our Lord Jesus Christ, to Your praise and glory. Amen.

Response

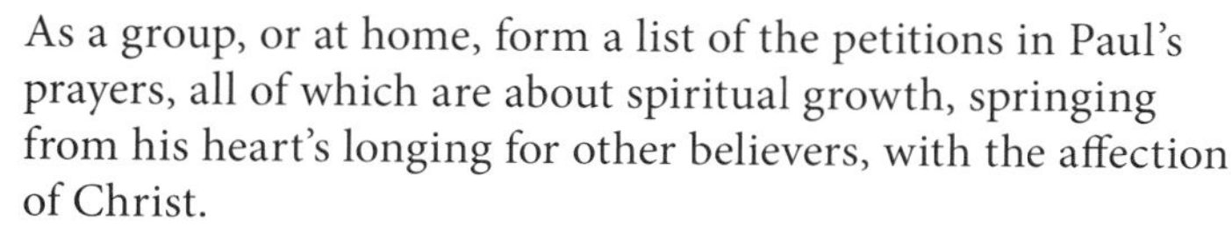

As a group, or at home, form a list of the petitions in Paul's prayers, all of which are about spiritual growth, springing from his heart's longing for other believers, with the affection of Christ.

Start here in Philippians chapter 1, separating some of the phrases: for example, that:

- their love may abound more and more in knowledge and depth of insight
- they may have discernment about what is vital
- they may grow in holy living until the day of Christ.

Then go in turn to Ephesians 1:15–19, Ephesians 3:16–19 and Colossians 1:9–12.

There will be some overlap, but you should end with a fair list of petitions.

Take the list home if you have done this as a group.

At home in your personal prayer rota I suggest you put down the names of believers in your fellowship, spread through Monday to Friday. If the fellowship is big perhaps use a monthly rota. Then, week one, or month one, pray for them with the first petition on the list, week two (or month two) the second one, and so on. Now you are being Pauline both in a regular pattern of remembering others and also of focusing on and prioritising their spiritual growth. Of course, pray the same petitions for yourself. I believe that such prayer is so Biblical that we will assuredly see results to God's glory.

I know some groups that issue a slip of paper to remind the members which petition to use each week or month. For many, prayer will be moved on to a far more purposeful and Biblical level, with the affection of Christ.

STUDY | **THREE**

Living is Christ

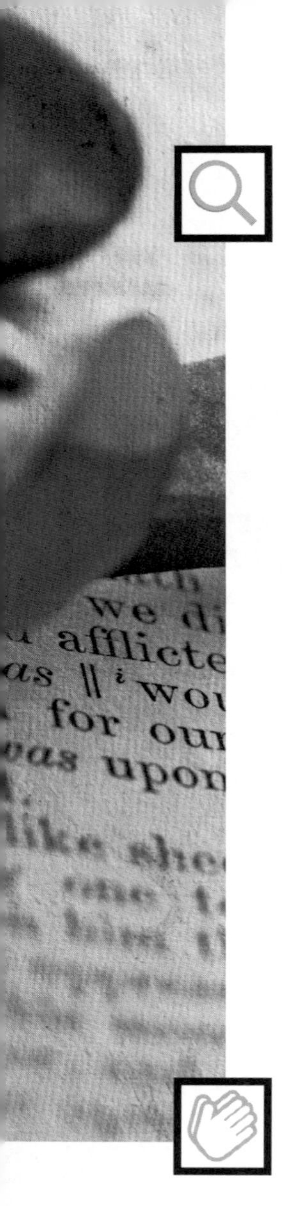

Focusing

Imagine yourself on a railway platform waiting for a train. What is your over-riding concern about this train? Design? Whether there is a seat? Your primary concern will be its destination – the purpose of its journey – and that it will get you there.

For Paul the priority purpose of the Christian life was clear. The old Spiritual expressed it well:

> The gospel train's a-coming, I hear it close at hand ...
> Get on board, little children, get on board. There's room for many a-more,
> The fare is cheap and all can go, the rich and poor are there,
> No second class aboard that train, no difference in the fare ...
> Get on board, little children, get on board ...
> O sinner, you're for ever lost if once you're left behind ...
> Get on board!

There's no doubt that what mattered most to the workers in the cotton fields was preaching the gospel.

In the first passage today we see that everything in Paul's life was geared to that gospel priority (and what he expects to be the primary concern of all believers and all churches). It is a concern that over-rides personal status and comfort; that puts suffering in perspective.

Opening Prayer

Gracious Lord, You see us as we really are; we cannot conceal any part of our life from You. So we ask that, as we study this passage today, we may be truly open to what Your Spirit shows us as relevant to our lives and that we may have sufficient grace to respond. Amen.

Bible Reading 1

Philippians 1:12-18; 27-28

[12]'Now I want you to know, brothers [and sisters], that what has happened to me has really served to advance the gospel. [13]As a result, it has become clear throughout the whole palace guard and to everyone else that I am in chains for Christ. [14]Because of my chains, most of the brothers in the Lord have been encouraged to speak the word of God more courageously and fearlessly.

[15]It is true that some preach Christ out of envy and rivalry, but others out of good will. [16]The latter do so in love, knowing that I am here for the defence of the gospel. [17]The former preach Christ out of selfish ambition, not sincerely, supposing that they can stir up trouble for me while I am in chains. [18]But what does it matter? The important thing is that in every way, whether from false motives or true, Christ is preached. And because of this I rejoice …

[27]Whatever happens, conduct yourselves in a manner worthy of the gospel of Christ. Then, whether I come and see you or only hear about you in my absence, I will know that you stand firm in one spirit, contending as one man for the faith of the gospel,[28]without being frightened in any way by those who oppose you.'

Reflection

Pick out the four times that 'gospel' is used in the verses above.

Then find the three times that 'preaching Christ' is used.

The whole passage is suffused with the passionate priority Paul has for the gospel of Christ.

Here is a man in prison, chained to a member of the Roman guard. There is not a breath of complaint, of self-pity or moaning. Whatever the circumstance in which he finds himself he seeks to turn them to witness; he turns problems into opportunities. The Philippians were no doubt very concerned and upset about his being in prison. So he

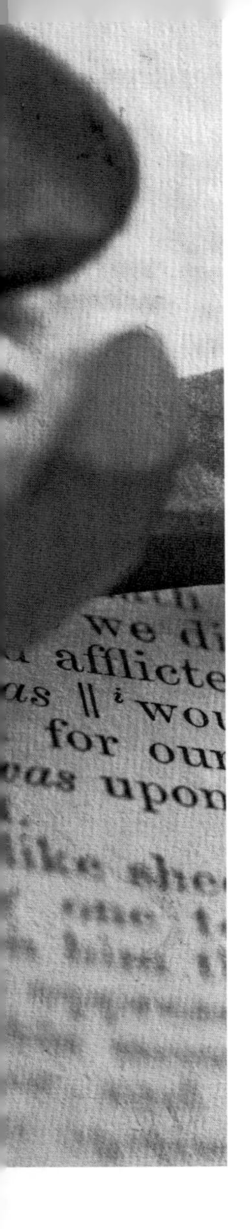

breathtakingly declares, '… what has happened to me has really served to advance the gospel'. The word 'advance' is a strong word. It could be used for an army cutting a way through a jungle or railway engineers cutting through a hill. The restrictive circumstances of his being in the power of the palace guard were cut through by Paul.

How were they cut through? What must have been obvious to his guards was that he was not bemoaning his fate but rising above his imprisonment with faith and joy (as he also did in prison in Philippi, Acts 16:25). Clearly Paul would also have prayed for his guards but the way he related to them must surely have had quite an impact.

When Nelson Mandela was imprisoned on Robben Island he and the others with him were treated as animals by most of the prison officers. In total contrast, Nelson treated them with politeness. He would say 'Goodnight, Mr ...' and 'Good morning, Mr ...' One warder was transformed by this; he later spoke of Nelson as 'B'wana, my friend'. This was the influence of a gracious man. So it must have been with Paul. It would have opened up conversations in the many hours that warders were chained to him. It became clear '… throughout the whole palace guard and to everyone else that I am in chains *[note the next words]* for Christ'. They did not just admire his courage; he showed them that what mattered most in his life was Christ.

In verse 27 he encourages the Philippians to conduct themselves '… in a manner worthy of the gospel of Christ'. He did; they should. Their lives mattered. Our lives matter. We are the shop window of the gospel in all circumstances. Paul realised that often it is fear that holds back our witness, and that is true today as opposition to Christians increases sharply. A young man came to see my son, a vicar in London. He was a Muslim, an Afghan asylum seeker, but he wanted to become a Christian. The reason? He had obtained work in an Aid agency in Kabul and was overwhelmed by the kindness he received from everyone there. He realised that they were all Christians and their love and care attracted him to Christ. When I asked a young lady, about to be confirmed in the faith, how she became a Christian, she pointed to a couple across the church and said, 'It was the way they took the cot death of their child that made me believe in God'.

Another result of Paul's courage is in verse 14: '... most of the brothers [and sisters] in the Lord have been encouraged to speak the word of God more courageously and fearlessly'. Great! I am thankful for the courageous witness and leadership of a number of Christians in my life who have encouraged me to act more boldly. But then (vv15–18) our breath is taken away – again! Imagine a situation where a group pulls out of your church and sets up a rival church right opposite your entrance. Or another church in the area seems far more successful at evangelising, especially drawing young people. What would your reaction be? Anger, jealousy, embarrassment, hurt? Paul here tells us of people preaching Christ out of selfish ambition, not sincerely, so that they can cause him trouble in prison. I feel my blood rising! But Paul rejoices! Yes, rejoices! Because the 'important thing' is that 'Christ is preached'.

In verse 27 he now encourages *them* to '... stand firm in one spirit, contending as one man for the faith of the gospel, *without being frightened in any way by those who oppose you* [my emphasis]' – the word for 'frightened' is the same as that used for the shying of a horse. That can be severely testing as, for instance, for Christians who were terribly tortured and killed by the Khmer Rouge. In the early church, Bp Ignatius was taken to martyrdom by ten guards 'like ten leopards' with their cruelty, but Ignatius showed them increasing kindness. Holding back on witnessing for Christ because of what others may think of us in the office or club or social group looks rather pathetic in comparison. Paul does not call us to dither but to 'contend' for the gospel – fearlessly yet graciously. The spreading of the gospel is a priority.

Discussion Starters

1. If anyone was drawn to Christ by the seeing the life of a Christian, please share. Discuss what particular aspects of a Christian's life attract others to Christ.

2. What in our lives as Christians might *de*tract others?

3. Does any circumstance frighten us about witnessing for Christ and the gospel? How can we face such fear? Of what are we actually afraid?

4. If another church is more successful evangelistically, do we react or can we overhaul our ways of witness to become more effective? What might need changing in our church's programme, publicity, buildings or in our personal attitudes to facilitate this?

Prayer

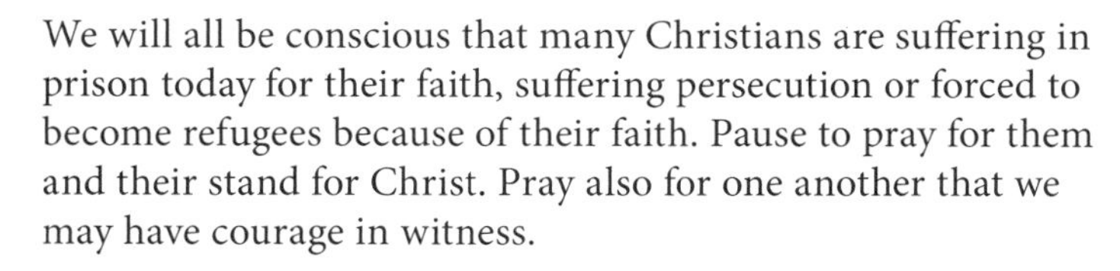

We will all be conscious that many Christians are suffering in prison today for their faith, suffering persecution or forced to become refugees because of their faith. Pause to pray for them and their stand for Christ. Pray also for one another that we may have courage in witness.

Worship

Sing or say together Charles Wesley's hymn *Jesus! the Name high over all.*

In the second reading we see Paul's commitment to exalt Christ in his life to the end of the line.

Bible Reading 2

Philippians 1:20–21

> [20]'I eagerly expect and hope that I will in no way be ashamed, but will have sufficient courage so that now as always Christ will be exalted in my body, whether by life or by death.[21]For to me, to live is Christ and to die is gain.'

Meditation

For the next 3–5 minutes, meditate individually in silence on these two verses, applying them personally.

Reflection

The immediate context of these verses is that Paul could be facing release or death. He thinks that through their prayers he will probably be delivered and he can see (v25) that this would help their progress and joy in the faith. But as the servant of Christ, he is open to *whatever* happens (so he does not decide what God should do and pray for it) and his priority is not

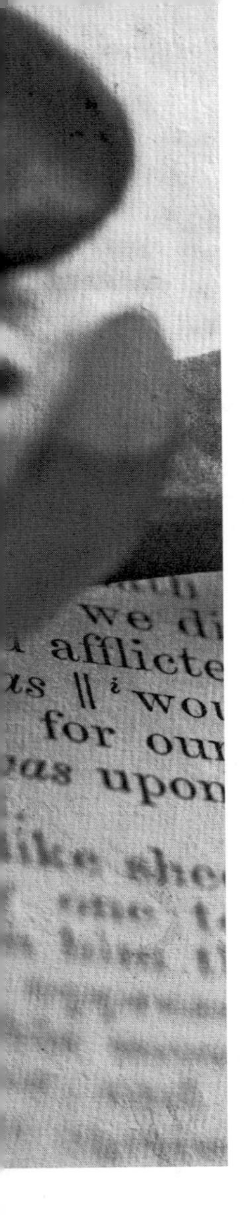

survival but that whether he is going to die or live *he will not let his Lord down.* He would be ashamed if he did. Instead he trusts he will have sufficient courage 'now as always' that '... Christ will be exalted in my body, whether by life or by death'. ('Exalt' is a word meaning 'magnify', not making something larger but enabling one to see something – in this case, Christ – more clearly.) Christ to be over all; exalting Christ always to be the priority of his life. Death has no fear: '... to depart and be with Christ ... is better by far ...' (v23). So the focus is on *how* he lives and *how* he dies – for Christ's sake and glory.

The witness of Christians dying can be very powerful when they seek to exalt Christ. Recently I was closely involved with a youngish mother dying of cancer. She had a clear Biblical view of suffering. Her radiance and peace were wonderful. She had a host of non-Christian friends and her emails to them were so moving and Christ-centred. She insisted that the Thanksgiving service for her should include a plea to all her friends who did not believe to come to a special Alpha course, just for them. She lived for Christ, right to the very end of the line.

There is usually no knowing how one might die, but we should pray that whatever happens we may (while our physical state makes it still possible) have grace to exalt Christ to our last breath.

But let's go a little deeper. Verse 21 says, 'For to me, to live is Christ ...'. We easily move on to 'to die is gain' but what does living for Christ involve? It is the overall purpose of our lives, far outweighing the importance of anything else in relationships, work, sport, achievement – anything. In the huge flurry of activity and demands upon us in this multi-media age, it is easy to have Christ as just part of our lives rather than as the one for whom we ultimately live. We can 'put on Christ' sincerely enough, but effectively take him off when not suitable.

When I was 18 I was conscripted into the army. On the first day we had to strip off our civilian clothes and put them in parcels addressed to our homes. We now had no choice but to wear uniform all day, every day, wherever we went. Yes, later we were allowed some civvies, but those first weeks meant we were immersed in soldiering. Living for Christ meant for Paul never removing the uniform. He saw baptism as dying with Christ and rising again with Him, once and for all, for life. We have 'put on the new self' and that means putting off the old (Eph. 4:22–24). It means seeking to put Christ first over everything; it means laying our life at His feet for His direction; it means checking and re-checking that we are still on track.

It can be costly. Years ago a missionary bishop, home from Africa, addressed undergraduates, pleading with them to see whether God was calling them to Africa. One undergraduate afterwards said to him, 'I could never live in Africa'. The bishop thundered back, 'I didn't ask you to live there but to die there!' In some baptismal services a cross is marked on the forehead with the words, 'Do not be ashamed to confess the faith of Christ crucified. Fight valiantly under the banner of Christ against sin, the world, and the devil, and continue His faithful soldier and servant *to the end of your life* [my emphasis]'. Yes, that is declaring 'to me, to live is Christ …'

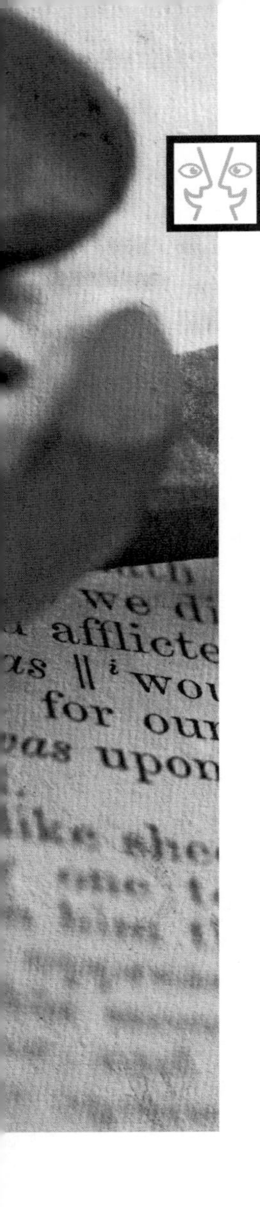

Discussion Starters

1. How can we help ourselves or one another to keep on track for Christ with our life, eg by a rule of life, through retreat or with the help of a spiritual director?

2. One fine Christian teacher said, 'We too easily turn to what we can get out of Christianity'. Are our prayers first for our self-preservation and benefit? How often do we pray for the advance of the gospel or for opportunities to witness to Christ?

3. Discuss how we can advance the gospel and speak of Christ to our friends in this materialistic and increasingly unbelieving world.

4. Have you been able, for example, to share love and care in bereavement, speaking of Christ when appropriate; or to show such love when others are suffering or lonely; or to give practical help showing love? Is showing love a way in for the gospel?

Closing Prayer

(To read alone or to say or sing together)

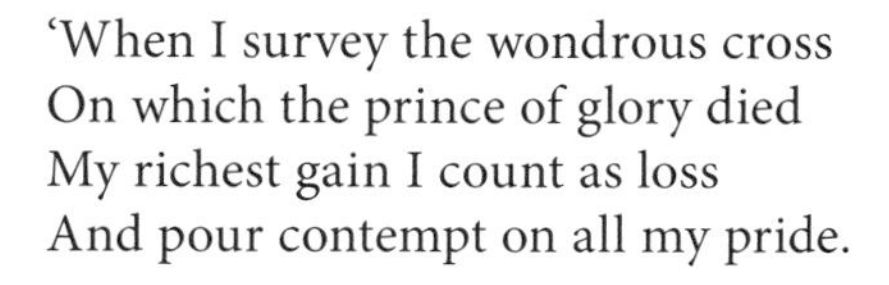

'When I survey the wondrous cross
On which the prince of glory died
My richest gain I count as loss
And pour contempt on all my pride.

Were the whole realm of nature mine,
That were an offering far too small
Love so amazing, so divine,
Demands my soul, my life, my all.'

Isaac Watts (1674–1748)

Mindset of Christ

Focusing

You have not been feeling well so you go to the doctor. He/she discerns what is wrong and then acts to get it sorted out so that you can return to full health.

The passage before us in this study is similar. Paul can praise much of what is happening in Philippi but he has discerned that there is a sickness in the midst and that this needs to be dealt with before the whole church is infected and made ineffective. The sickness is a lack of humility amongst some, especially leaders, as seen in chapter 4:2 with Euodia and Syntyche, leaders in the church.

It is very sad when church is used for personal ego-trips – the queen of the kitchen who has to have her way, the control-freak pastor, the resisters to change who only want what *they* like in church services or furniture, the 'I always decorate the lectern at Easter' person.

Paul tackles the situation in Philippi head-on. He can praise their gospel commitment and their generosity but not the way they seem to make more of others' weaknesses rather than their strengths. It is the reason for writing the letter. They need to relate to one another and the world with humility. Their failure to do so puts the church's life and witness in serious danger.

Opening Prayer

Gracious Lord, we are humbled by the truth that You laid aside Your majesty and came to this world in amazing humility, that You lived in simplicity and never wanted the earthly power or riches that humanity so often seeks above all else, that You humbly laid down Your life for us on the cross. As we share in this study, we pray that Your humility will be always in our minds and that we may be shown if we have acted without such humility in the church and, if so, may have the grace to change. For Your name's sake. Amen.

Bible Reading 1

Philippians 2:1-2

[1]'If you have any encouragement from being united with Christ, if any comfort from his love, if any fellowship with the Spirit, if any tenderness and compassion, [2]then make my joy complete by being like-minded, having the same love, being one in spirit and purpose.'

Reflection

United in Christ

How do you challenge others when their attitudes as a Christian are 'sick'? Paul's technique is to shame them into action by making them think of the huge benefits and blessings of being 'in Christ' (the NIV has 'united with Christ' to explain the phrase but the Greek is simply 'in Christ'). It is a phrase much used by Paul to express the radical change in our status when we turn to Him as our Saviour (eg 2 Cor. 5:17 '... if anyone is in Christ, he is a new creation; the old has gone, the new has come!'). When, it seems, some of the Philippians were concerned with their status as human beings, with selfish ambition, Paul presses the truth that we have, in Christ, the most precious status of all and any other status-seeking looks pathetic in comparison. So they should focus on living out their new status to the full.

He then points to some of the blessings. They know Christ's 'encouragement' (v1) which means his 'coming alongside' thus knowing He is with us and indwelling us. They know 'comfort from his love' – the many touches and hugs of His love and the supremely self-giving love of His death for our sins on the cross. They know the 'fellowship with the Spirit', the church as a community of the Spirit, united by the fact that every true believer has been born again of the Spirit, sharing this same birthright; that the Spirit inspires, convicts, teaches, gifts, moulds; that He directs the church; they will know the many times they have received 'tenderness and compassion'.

So, he argues, if you know all these blessings, you should be

'like-minded' (v2). We are to have 'the same love' (v2). This is a love that 'comforts' (v1) a word that has the idea of reaching out to others with a gentle but definite influence, consoling and encouraging. It means going to others who may think differently from us and seeking in love to explain why we think as we do and then listening to them. Think how Jesus acted with Peter on the beach after his denial (John 21:15), with the Emmaus two (Luke 24:13) and with Martha at the death of Lazarus (John 11:17) – all very personal. Love may be rejected but we must still offer it. Indeed, there is to be 'tenderness and compassion' (v1), and the words imply that it is to come from the very depths of our being – nothing shallow or false.

We also saw that 'encouragement' (v1) means 'coming alongside'. Our Lord came alongside all sorts of people, even the twisting tax-collectors and prostitutes, so we have no excuse to avoid coming alongside others with whom we are 'one in Christ' because we do not like them (which was probably the case in Philippi). When I was at Theological College we were all part of a Prayer Partnership scheme. Each week we arranged a time to pray with another person on the list. The names were in two columns so as one column moved down each week you could see that someone you did not like was getting nearer! But then, when you met to pray and learned more about that person you realised how wrong your impressions had been.

In verse 2 'being one in spirit and purpose' is what Christ calls us to be like, working with Him, and for Him and His kingdom, not for our own ends. Their divisions were not 'being one in spirit'. Galatians 5:16–17 starkly states that dissensions, factions and envy are from our sinful nature and are contrary to the Spirit, whereas verses 22–23 say that life in the Spirit will show the fruit of '… love, joy, peace, patience, kindness, goodness, faithfulness, gentleness and self-control'. So we need to work and pray for the work of the Spirit among us to change us more and more to be in fellowship with the Spirit.

The Spirit is also the director of the church and the Apostles were very conscious of this. In Acts 13:2 the Spirit directs the sending out of Barnabas and Saul and in Acts 15:28

the momentous decisions of the Council of Jerusalem are introduced as 'It seemed good to the Holy Spirit and to us …' This is what should be so in every church council. So Philippians 2:2 says we are to be a church '… one in spirit and in purpose', pulling together for Christ and not against one another, constantly praying: 'Lord, what is your will for us as a church?'

Discussion Starters

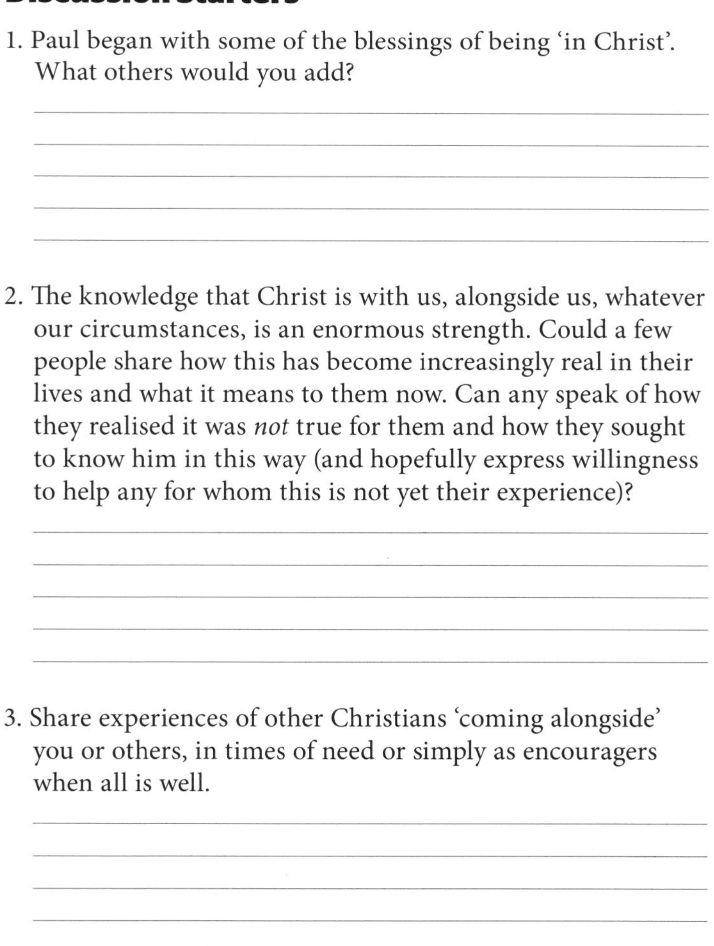

1. Paul began with some of the blessings of being 'in Christ'. What others would you add?

2. The knowledge that Christ is with us, alongside us, whatever our circumstances, is an enormous strength. Could a few people share how this has become increasingly real in their lives and what it means to them now. Can any speak of how they realised it was *not* true for them and how they sought to know him in this way (and hopefully express willingness to help any for whom this is not yet their experience)?

3. Share experiences of other Christians 'coming alongside' you or others, in times of need or simply as encouragers when all is well.

Worship

Read together or sing (at least verses 1 and 4) Stuart Townend and Keith Getty's hymn *In Christ Alone*, to give thanks for the blessings of being 'in Christ'.

Bible Reading 2

Philippians 2:3-5

[3]'Do nothing out of selfish ambition or vain conceit, but in humility consider others better than yourselves. [4]Each of you should look not only to your own interests, but also to the interests of others. [5]Your attitude [mindset] should be the same as that of Christ Jesus.'

Reflection

Humility?

Verses 3 and 4 show what can often happen in secular groups, workplaces, clubs, sport, education – ambition only for yourself, vain conceit and looking only to your own interests. 'Live for number one' is the philosophy of millions.

In contrast, all who are 'in Christ' should be clearly different, marked by humility.

In the world of Paul's day, humility was despised. It meant those who served you or cringers, cowards or weak people of no value. But in the Bible the word is transformed. To be truly humble you need strength, to resist self-serving tendencies. To be a great tennis player, for instance, and to be able to praise another player who is clearly better, takes the strength of humility. A truly humble person is not wet, weak or a doormat. Moses, a great leader for God, is described as '… more humble than anyone else on … earth' (Num. 12:3).

A proud person in the church will always cause friction but a humble person is a peace-maker. So Paul writes (vv3–4) '… consider others better than yourselves' and '… look not only to your own interests, but also to the interests of others'. Such a Christian is a gem and where this is a dominant spirit in the church, dissension fades away.

Discussion Starters

1. Why do envy, jealousy of others' position and denigrating others' faith or lifestyle sometimes arise in a church? Paul exposed it, but are we sometimes too soft about exposing it, so that it festers, damaging the gospel witness of the church?

2. Discuss the phrases 'consider others better than yourselves' and 'looking to the interests of others'.

3. I once asked a lady why she had started coming to a particular church. She replied, 'Because I was met by love'. Others have gone to a church as a stranger, been welcomed with a handshake but then ignored at the end of the service and never returned. How do you think welcoming love should be expressed and evident?

Response

The Model of Humility

Verse 5: Paul has done his best to tackle the problems in the church, caused by those who lacked humility, and he has urged realistic action. But now he gives the *coup de gras* by making them look in wonderful detail at their Lord and Saviour. He is *the* example of humility. They should aim to have his 'attitude' or mindset. So must we.

Verses 6–11 form one of the precious gems of the New Testament. It is not here to teach theology (although it does). It is here as *the* illustration of humility. It is almost certainly a hymn. Paul intends us to grasp its broad sweep, first (vv6–10) of what our Lord did and, by implication, how we should follow; then (vv9–11) what God did.

So I am keen that we should primarily meditate on it and I hope you will find it helpful to see the remarkable alignment with John 13, where the truths of this hymn are expressed in practice (some think the hymn is a meditation on John 13). Please split into two groups: group A to read the verses from John 13 and group B the verses from Philippians, alternating throughout, with a short pause between each double reading to meditate.

GROUP A – John chapter 13	GROUP B – Philippians chapter 2
[3]'Jesus knew that the Father had put all things under his power, and that he had come from God and was returning to God;	[6]'[Christ Jesus], who, being in very nature God, did not consider equality with God something to be grasped,
[4]so he got up from the meal [and] took off his outer clothing,	[7]but made himself nothing,
and wrapped a towel round his waist. [5]After that, he poured water into a basin and began to wash his disciples' feet, drying them with the towel that was wrapped around him.'	taking the very nature of a servant, being made in human likeness. [8]And being found in appearance as a man, he humbled himself and became obedient to death – even death on a cross!
[12]'When he had finished washing their feet, he put on his clothes and returned to his place.'	[9]Therefore God exalted him to the highest place
[13]"You call me 'Teacher' and 'Lord' and rightly so, for that is what I am."	and gave him the name that is above every name, [10]that at the name of Jesus every knee should bow, in heaven and on earth and under the earth, and every tongue confess that Jesus Christ is Lord, to the glory of God the Father.'

Meditation

I suggest that for the next few minutes you meditate individually on this Model of Humility. It is significant that the 'vain conceit' of Philippians 2:3 is actually 'empty glory' in the Greek; and in verse 7 the contrast of our Lord's humility is rammed home as the same word for 'empty' is used, but for Christ it is *emptying himself of the glory* and the privileges of the Godhead (but not of his divinity).

You might like to note also that humility involved obedience to the Cross as the will and purpose of His Father (v8).

Reflect on how we might apply what we have considered to ourselves.

Response

The punch line in John 13 is 'I have set you an example that you should do as I have done for you' (v15). Yes, an example to *us*. In Philippians 2, Paul also expects a response – read verses 12–18.

If there is time, share the fruits of your meditation on these passages. If time has gone, write them down when you get home but, either way, make special time today to pray that your life may change as a result.

Worship

Say together or sing (at least) verses 1, 3 and 5 of the hymn *At the name of Jesus* (Caroline M. Noel).

Closing Prayer

I ask the group leader to pray, rather than my writing a prayer, as she/he will be able to encapsulate what God has been doing with the group in this study.

Knowing Christ

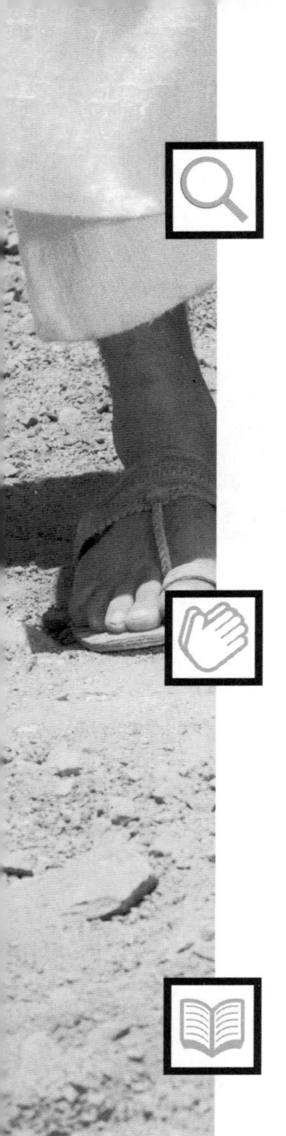

Focusing

How much do you really know about others in the room?

(The group leader will now give directions for a gentle activity, the purpose of which is to affirm that the more time we spend with someone, the more we know them. Details can be found in Study Five of the Leader's Notes).

In our study today that is precisely the point of Paul's passionate writing. He wants to know Christ more and, from our angle, if we were asked a string of questions about our Lord, we would no doubt see that our knowledge is only partial. There is clearly so much more to know and this only comes when we have a burning desire to **know Him**.

Opening Prayer

(using part of the prayer in Col. 1:9-14)

Gracious Lord, we ask You to fill us with the knowledge of Your will through all spiritual wisdom and understanding. And we pray this in order that we may live lives worthy of You and may please You in every good work, growing in our knowledge of You. So will You please open our hearts and our minds to know You more as we study Your word today. For Your name's sake. Amen.

Bible Reading 1

Philippians 3:7-9

[7]'But whatever was to my profit I now consider loss for the sake of Christ. [8]What is more, I consider everything a loss compared to the surpassing greatness of knowing Christ Jesus my Lord, for whose sake I have lost all things. I consider them rubbish, that I may gain Christ [9] and be found in him, not having a righteousness of my own that comes from the law, but that which is through faith in Christ – the righteousness that comes from God and is by faith.'

Reflection

Verses 7–9 are a divine Profit and Loss Account, but whereas a financial account has to *reduce* losses to increase gains, the divine one has to *increase* losses to increase gains!

Loss. A skim-reading might indicate setting aside our earthly position, eg our scholastic achievements, our career successes or our position in society, but that would only be so if it became the elephant in the room, obscuring our priority for Christ (like the rich young ruler in Luke 18:18–22 who therefore was told to sell all he had).

But the meaning here in Philippians 3 is about everything on which we may have relied for our salvation. In Paul's case it was the keeping of every bit of the law and the huge number of rules. When Christ met him and he grasped the glorious truth of salvation by faith it was a totally new dimension; all the powers and position he had as a Pharisee became as nothing and he saw them as garbage. They could not compare with the '… surpassing greatness of knowing Christ Jesus my Lord …' (v8). ('Knowing' is not just head knowledge but the inner spirit, too. It is a word for intimacy, as in marriage).

Is this relevant to us? For some it certainly is. There are many caught up in religiosity, in dependence on works, in reliance on going to church or having been baptised, who have not grasped the gospel, like a university undergraduate who listened to a full explanation of the gospel of salvation by faith in Christ, and then said, 'I see I must try harder'! I recall a church member in Manchester whose husband died and in bereavement ministry she came to trust Jesus. She later stood in front of the Parochial Church Council and said, 'I have been in this church for fifty-six years, and on the Council for many years, yet only now can I say "I know Jesus"'.

Gain. In verses 8–9 '… that I may gain Christ …' is geared, you will see, to salvation by faith in Christ. The 'righteousness' that comes from God is not some blanket of goodness that makes us perfect, it means 'being right with God'. In Romans 5:1–2 he writes, '… since we have been justified through faith, we have peace with God through our Lord Jesus Christ …'

It is a gift. It is free. Isn't it wonderful? But when we 'gain' the intimacy of a person, as in marriage or close friendships, we benefit from their gifts, character, insights, learning and so much more. Paul, writing in Colossians 2:2–3, wants believers to '... have the full riches of complete understanding, in order that they may know the mystery of God, namely, Christ, *in whom are hidden all the treasures of wisdom and knowledge* [my emphasis]'. And in 1 Corinthians 3:22–23 he declares: '... all are yours, and you are of Christ, and Christ is of God'. So the scope of 'knowing Christ' is vast.

Worship

Share together what it means to you to have 'gained' Christ; the blessings and joys that this has brought you. Perhaps some could share how they needed to rid themselves of the 'earning salvation by good works' idea.

Then sing or say together the hymn by Graham Kendrick *Knowing You* which begins 'All I once held dear' and is based on this passage of Philippians 3.

Bible Reading 2

Philippians 3:10-11

[10]'I want to know Christ and the power of his resurrection and the fellowship of sharing in his sufferings, becoming like him in his death, [11]and so, somehow, to attain to the resurrection from the dead.'

Reflection

I want to know Christ

When, some years ago, I spent several months digging into this letter, it was this verse that leapt from the page and penetrated my heart. It has reverberated for me ever since. Here is a man of senior years, of brilliant intelligence, of a second-to-none understanding of the gospel and a deep relationship to his Saviour, who still wants to know Christ more. 'I WANT!' – it would seem that he never lost that burning passion.

Many years ago I was speaking at a convention in Australia and afterwards an elderly clergyman, aged ninety-three, came up to me and grasped my hands and said, with tears running down his face, 'Thank you, thank you for what you have taught me of Jesus tonight'. I was overwhelmed, humbled and stunned. Would I still want to know more of Christ in old age? Since then I have seen Christians, even ministers, lose that passion in later years, and yet others growing more passionate. What about you?

Discussion Starter

What are the differences between *wishing* to do something and *wanting* to do it, eg slimming, oil-painting, winning an Olympic medal for swimming? Apply your ideas to 'I want to know Christ'.

Response

And, if we want to know Him more, what do we do about it? Here's a check-list:

- We ought to pray that we may know Him more and more and this should be a constant prayer on our lips and in our hearts. Do we? If not, get sorted!
- We should hunger to learn more of Him through our reading of the New Testament, meditating, pondering and reflecting on the gospels in detail. Do we? It is vital for survival.
- We should take time to be alone with Him every day if possible but, if not, set time in our diary to go and be away from everyone so that we can let the dust settle and speak with Him, asking Him also to show us areas of our life that do not honour Him. Do we?

Share your experiences of these ways and add to this check-list other ways in which you have been enabled to know Him more.

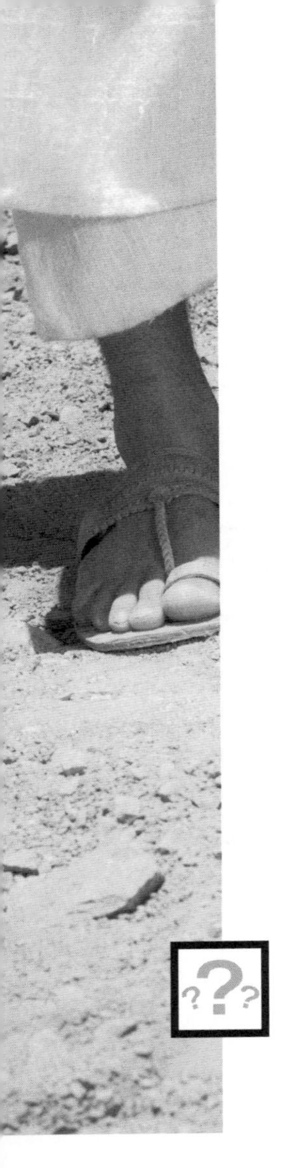

When wanting to know '... the power of his resurrection and the fellowship of his sufferings ...', it is best to take these together for they are part of a whole. Dying to sin and rising to new life are always part and parcel of the same truth, as they were in our Lord's death and rising. It seems that, for Paul, the more he enters into the understanding of Christ's sufferings, particularly when he suffers as a Christian, the more he knows power and new life in Christ. In 2 Corinthians 1:5 he writes, 'For just as the sufferings of Christ flow over into our lives, so also through Christ our comfort overflows'. Amy Carmichael of Dohnavur inspired many others by her meditative writings and she would say that when she suffered it was 'a chance to die' to self and to be thrown more on to Christ's grace and power.

In 2 Corinthians 4:8–10 Paul writes of being '... hard pressed on every side ... perplexed ... persecuted ... struck down ...' and each phrase is matched by a **but**: **but** not crushed, **but** not in despair, **but** not abandoned, **but** not destroyed. He then explains: 'We always carry around in our body the death of Jesus, so that the life of Jesus may also be revealed in our body'. So in Philippians 3:10 we see that identifying with Christ more closely in His death and resurrection is a way to be more like Him, and verse 11 shows Paul wanting the risen life in Him to be increasingly attuned to life beyond the grave.*

Discussion Starters

1. What does this passage mean to you? Can some people share how they or others have been brought closer to Christ by suffering, or have been helped by suffering to alter their values and see with Christ's eyes what is really valuable about life?

2. How do we get more to the heart of Christ's sufferings for us on the cross? If you saw Mel Gibson's 2004 film *The Passion* did you find the stark depiction of our Lord's sufferings too difficult to watch or has it forever brought, for example, the thirty-nine lashes to vivid reality? Paul understood it only too well, as he tells us in 2 Corinthians 11:24 'Five times I received from the Jews the forty lashes minus one'.

Share what has helped you to enter more into the suffering of our Lord – for instance, I recall the impact of going to a Good Friday three-hour service for the first time – a wonderful three hours of devotion, teaching and meditation. I also recall the impact of hearing J.S. Bach's *St John Passion*, reading a book on the cross, meditating on Psalm 22 and, of course, on the gospel accounts, and going to the Oberammergau Passion Play – and you?

3. What do you think are marks of 'knowing' the power of Christ's resurrection in a Christian's life?

Worship

Say or sing together the hymn *Oh to See the Dawn* by Stuart Townend and Keith Getty.

Bible Reading 3

Philippians 3:12–14

[12]'Not that I have already obtained all this, or have already been made perfect, but I press on to take hold of that for which Christ Jesus took hold of me. [13]Brothers [and sisters], I do not consider myself yet to have taken hold of it. But one thing I do: Forgetting what is behind and straining towards what is ahead, [14]I press on towards the goal to win the prize for which God has called me heavenwards in Christ Jesus.'

Reflection

As a boy I went with a friend to ask for a holiday job with a farmer. He told us to go to a field (it was enormous!) and start weeding. He said he would come later in the day to inspect. We worked hard. He didn't come. Same next day and the next. On the fourth day we were lying out in the sun, having only done a small section of weeding, when he came. That was it.

Jesus told parables like that. Going on to the end is a mark of dedication. A non-Christian correspondent of a major UK newspaper recently wrote after a visit to Africa that the only hope for Africa was with Christians as they did not give up. Why don't they?

What a difference there is between aiming for an award and aiming to please a person. When I was conscripted into the army we were inspired by a fatherly Irish Sergeant Major. When we came to the passing-out parade, we all wanted to do our very best, not for the army but for him, and we were devastated when a howling wind meant that half of us did not hear his order to about-turn. We had failed *him*.

In 2 Corinthians 5:9 Paul says '... we make it our goal to

please him ...' [my emphasis]. In Philippians 3 he writes, '... one thing I do ...' is a task *for Christ*, that for which Christ took hold of him. So Paul will press on at it to the end. Elsewhere he encourages young Timothy to see Christian service like being a soldier: 'Endure hardship with us like a good soldier of Christ Jesus. No-one serving as a soldier gets involved in civilian affairs – he wants to please his commanding officer' (2 Tim. 2:3).

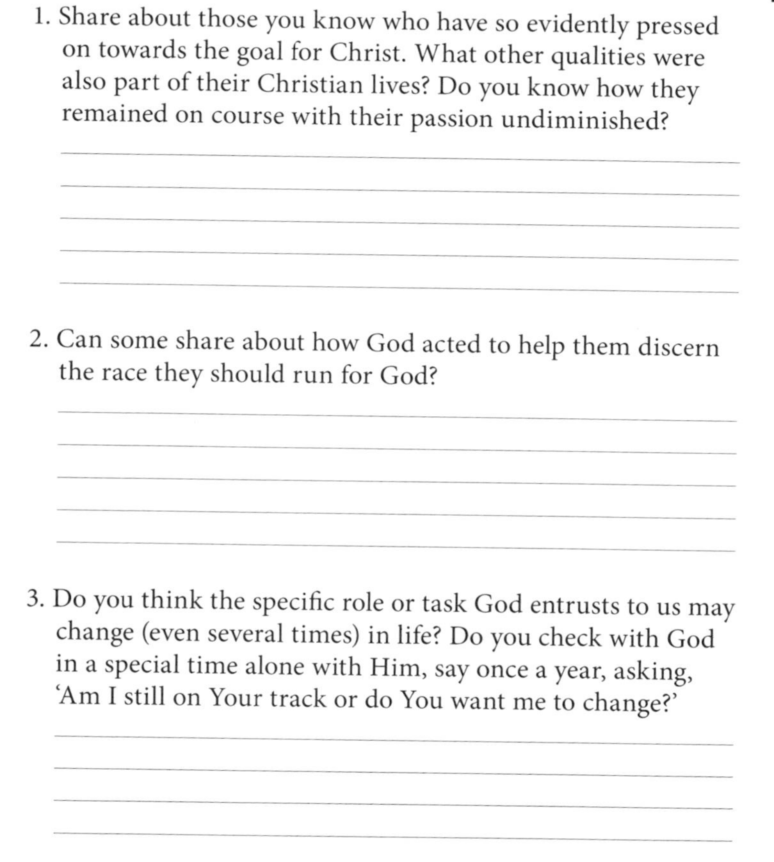

Discussion Starters

1. Share about those you know who have so evidently pressed on towards the goal for Christ. What other qualities were also part of their Christian lives? Do you know how they remained on course with their passion undiminished?

2. Can some share about how God acted to help them discern the race they should run for God?

3. Do you think the specific role or task God entrusts to us may change (even several times) in life? Do you check with God in a special time alone with Him, say once a year, asking, 'Am I still on Your track or do You want me to change?'

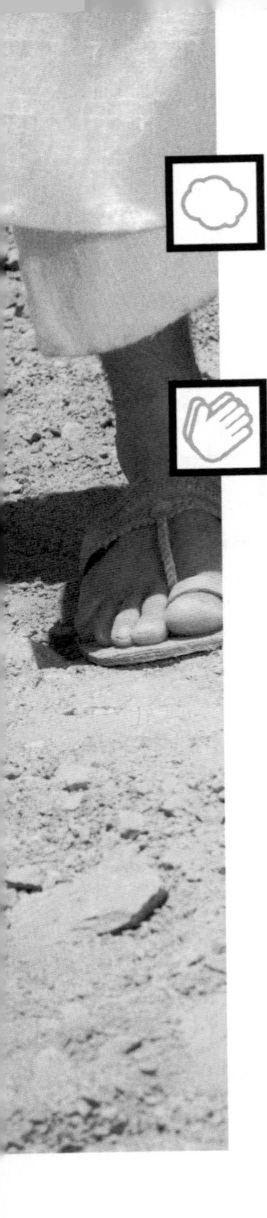

Meditation

Much of this study requires a personal response. I suggest that after completing it you take time to read Matthew 5–7, measuring your life, verse by verse, against the life of the One you *want* to know and to be like.

Closing Prayer

O God, light of the minds that know You,
life of the souls that love You,
strength of the thoughts that seek You,
Help us to know You, that we may truly love You,
to love You that we may fully serve You,
whose service is perfect freedom. Amen.

*In his book *The One Big Question* published by CWR, the author considers the issue of suffering in greater depth. To purchase a copy visit www.cwr.org.uk or a Christian bookshop.

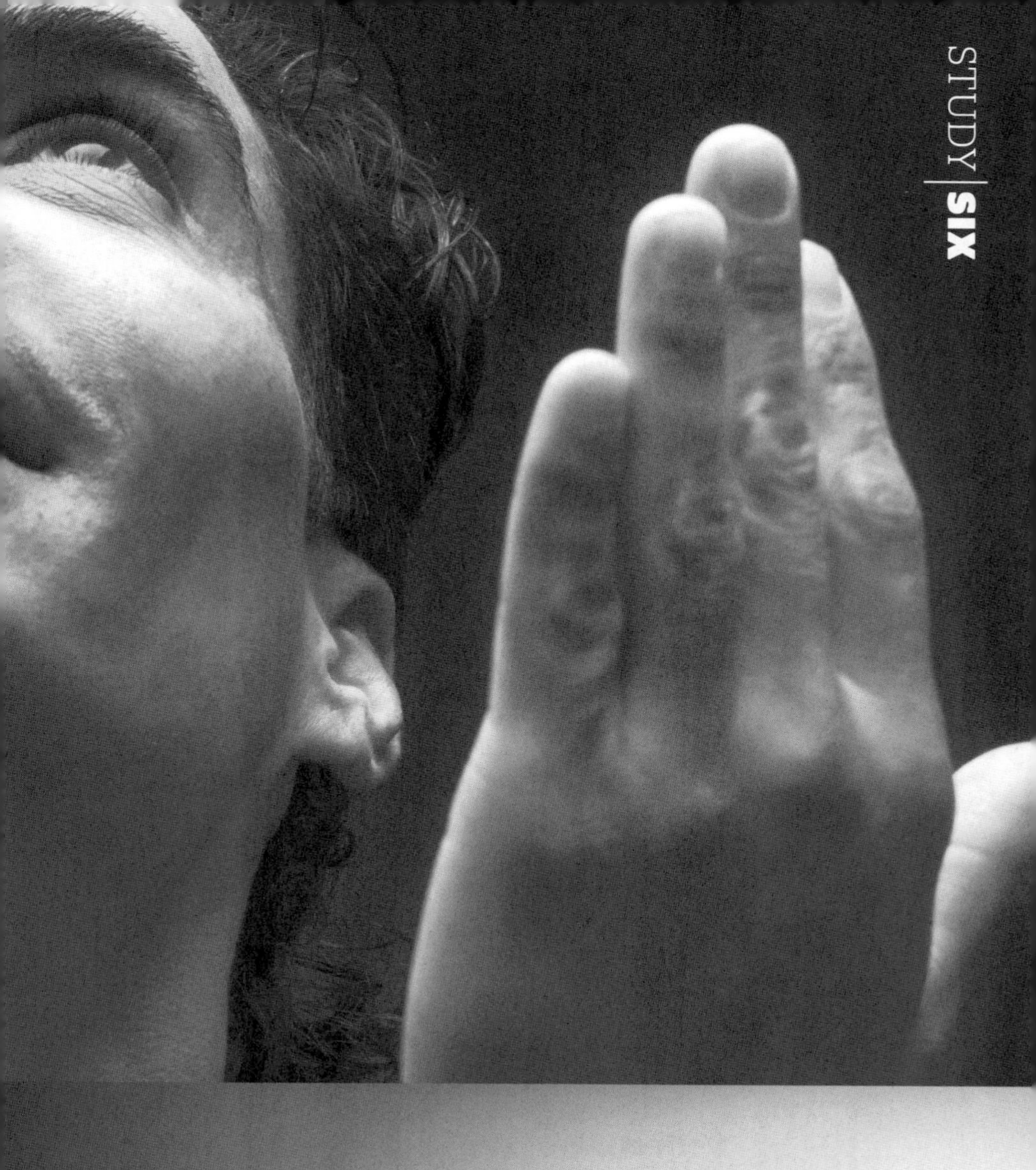

Rejoicing in Christ

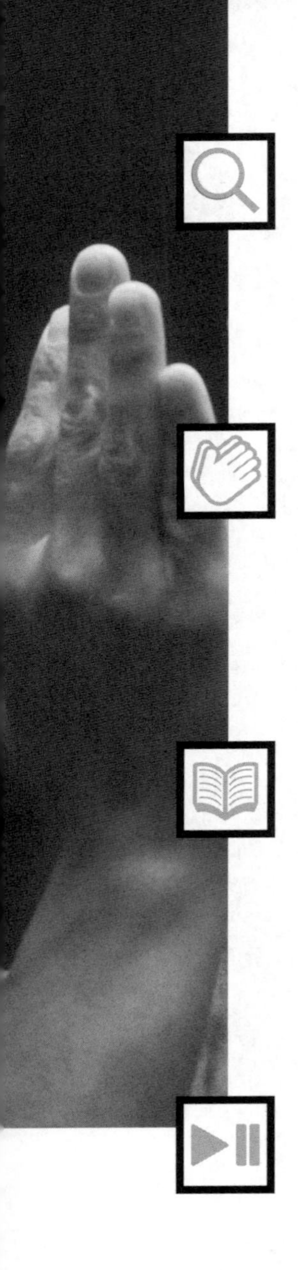

Focusing

As the ship edges forwards towards the port through a rough sea, hazardous rocks can be seen and the entrance to the port seems very narrow. Time to get anxious? No, because we have picked up the port's pilot and he knows every hazard. The unusual course the ship is steering is obviously under his control. So we do not worry about the situation. We trust the pilot.

Opening Prayer

Gracious Lord, that You came amongst us in human form and that You loved us so much that You went to the cross for our salvation is overwhelmingly wonderful. We can never thank You enough. We pray that we may increasingly live as You want us to live, setting aside empty ambitions and self-centredness, and living in humility with You as our focus, our joy, our example and, in all things, our pilot and Lord. Amen.

Bible Reading 1

Philippians 4:4-7

[4]'Rejoice in the Lord always. I will say it again: Rejoice! [5]Let your gentleness be evident to all. The Lord is near. [6]Do not be anxious about anything, but in everything, by prayer and petition, with thanksgiving, present your requests to God. [7]And the peace of God, which transcends all understanding, will guard your hearts and minds in Christ Jesus.'

Reflection

The Peace of a Humble Christ-centred Life

The sun has come out! After the exposures of what is wrong, and the instructions of Paul's letter, we have a sunset ending; the glow of a life with hearts centred on our Lord, our self-interest back into perspective and true satisfaction in living the way of our Lord. It is positive Christianity!

'Rejoice in the Lord always. I will say it again: Rejoice!' (v4) has special connotations for Myrtle and me. In our first three years of ministry Myrtle was in hospital seven times. We established the habit of saying this verse together as the ambulance bell grew nearer. It has remained special throughout our life, not least in times when our ministry was under pressure. So when I expounded this letter at the Keswick convention I repeated several times, 'Rejoice in the Lord, *not in circumstances*'. It shot through one man's heart and remained there daily from then on. A few months later his wife was killed outright on a pedestrian crossing. When the police came to tell him, the text shot into his mind and, in spite of his grief, he had deep peace. He felt the Lord had prepared the way.

Why the 'again' and 'always'? George Herbert said that Paul doubles it to take away the scruples of those who might say: 'What, shall we rejoice in affliction?' We do not rejoice about the affliction but rejoice that the Lord is with us whatever may happen to us.

We are to rejoice in the Lord because, although everything else changes, *He* never changes; He is the same yesterday, today and for ever (Heb. 13:8). He is our Saviour for ever; His promises are not broken; His love for us cannot change; He is faithful. Suffering so easily consumes Christians if they have not rid themselves of the view that God only exists to make us happy, or if they ask the sad question, 'Why has this happened to me?' as if God is some schoolmaster dishing out punishments and rewards. The truth of our being His for ever gets smothered.

Paul faces this out in Romans 8, showing the necessity of grasping the truth of our being children of God for ever, then contrasting sufferings with the glory ahead and rejoicing that nothing can separate us from the love of God in Christ Jesus. When sick or dying believers are so clearly able to rejoice in the Lord, keeping suffering in perspective, it is a wonderful witness.

One result from rejoicing in the Lord always is not being 'pushy' to get one's way; not saying, 'Me first', but having a 'gentleness' (v5) that is 'evident to all'. This is the witness of

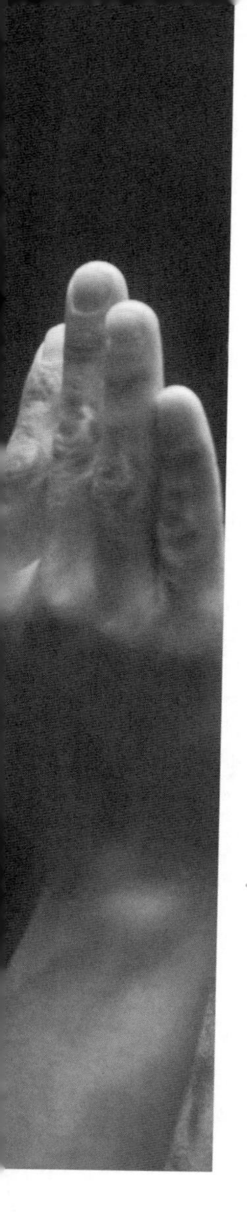

a lovely spirit. The word is also translated as 'magnanimity', a 'big-heartedness', 'kindness', 'merciful'; not insisting on one's rights; someone who has a welcoming face. There is no strictness and hardness; it is someone living out the truth of James 2:13: 'Mercy triumphs over judgment!' Adding 'the Lord is near' in Philippians 4:5 may be a reminder of how all this is true of His dealings with *us*.

When we 'rejoice in the Lord always' we have no reason to be 'anxious about anything'. Oswald Chambers called worry an 'unconscious blasphemy'. We need to pause and digest this. So much worry and anxiety is unnecessary. For example, we are being sent for a scan or a test and start worrying, losing sleep and thinking the worst but the scan shows all is clear. Our child starts at a new school and we worry all day, which does not benefit the child, change their day or leave us in the best state to welcome him or her back at the end of the day. We worried about what *might* be wrong rather than what *is* wrong. I like the Chinese man who said: 'Don't worry at night as you will lose sleep. Don't worry by day or your work will suffer. Don't worry at mealtimes as it will affect you digestion. Decide on a time to worry, then sit down with your Bible and the worry will have gone!' In other words, face the worry head on and ask yourself why you are worrying. Our Lord said: (Matt. 6:34) '… do not worry about tomorrow, for tomorrow will worry about itself. Each day has enough trouble of its own.'

But, we might say, Jesus agonised in the Garden of Gethsemane. Yes, but He did not worry. He brought His petition to his Father and He wanted most of all to do His Father's will. That was His burning concern. So here in verse 6 we are to 'present' our 'requests to God'. We slip into His presence and tell Him what we are facing. We do not tell Him what to do. His will and purpose are far greater than ours. We come as a child to a parent, we tell Him what is on our heart and we do so in a spirit of 'thanksgiving'. It means we trust Him. Peter tells us (1 Peter 5:6–7) to humble ourselves under the mighty hand of God, so that '… he may lift you up in due time', and then adds: 'Cast all your anxiety on him because he cares for you.' It is a marvellous relief when we deliberately bring a problem to our Lord, place it in His hands and leave it with Him. Worry disappears!

So then the outcome in Philippians 4:7 is '… the peace of God, which transcends all understanding, will guard your hearts and your minds in Christ Jesus'. Recently a great servant of God was diagnosed with terminal cancer. He and his wife laid this before God. They did not *demand* healing but entrusted the whole situation to God. They wrote a few weeks later that for the first time in their lives they had really come to know the deep reality of that peace which passes understanding. The key? Their focus on Christ. They rejoice in the Lord always. Myrtle and I were particularly overwhelmed with this peace a few years ago when we were about to crash-land in Zimbabwe. Our hearts and minds were truly *guarded*.

An example of Paul practising what he preached is found in 2 Corinthians 12:8–9 where Paul brings his physical suffering to the Lord: 'Three times I pleaded with the Lord to take it away from me. But he said to me, "My grace is sufficient for you, for my power is made perfect in weakness". Therefore I will boast all the more gladly about my weaknesses, so that Christ's power may rest on me.' Here he turns to the Lord, he brings his requests, he sees that God's glory and purpose are not to be in healing but in the witness of sufficient grace. He then does not just put up with it but boasts (v10 'delights') in his weaknesses. He rejoices in the Lord.

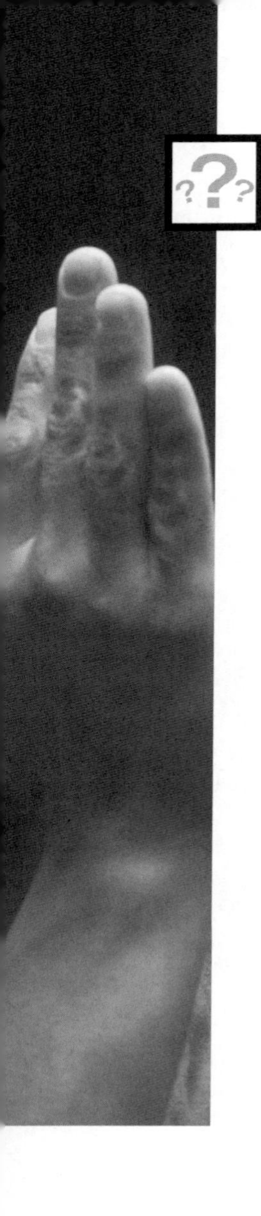

Discussion Starters

1. Have there been times when you have felt angry with God instead of rejoicing? What do you think causes us to be angry? Is it that we want Him to do our will or give us what we want and He doesn't? How have you grown into being more trusting whatever happens in life?

2. Can you recall moments of magnanimity by our Lord in the New Testament or in His parables and other teaching? Do you know believers who have outstandingly shown magnanimity to you or to others? How might you be more like that?

3. Do you agree that many non-believers think the church has a 'no' image rather than a 'yes' one? If so, how can we change, as a church and as individual Christians, to have more of a 'yes-face' image?

4. Have you been able to face your worries head-on and been able to *leave* them in Christ's hands?

Worship

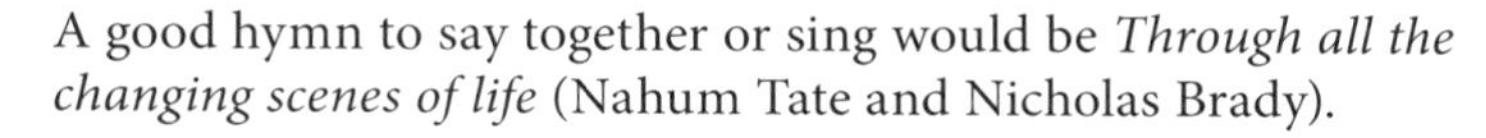

A good hymn to say together or sing would be *Through all the changing scenes of life* (Nahum Tate and Nicholas Brady).

Bible Reading 2

Philippians 4:12–13

[12]'I know what it is to be in need, and I know what it is to have plenty. I have learned the secret of being content in any and every situation, whether well fed or hungry, whether living in plenty or in want. [13]I can do everything through him who gives me strength.'

Reflection

A Practical Example of Humble Living

Discussion about worry may well have included worry about money and possessions. Paul makes a remarkable statement in verse 12. He has known plenty and has known need. In 2 Corinthians 11:27 he writes: 'I have laboured and toiled and have often gone without sleep; I have known hunger and thirst and have often gone without food; I have been cold and naked.' It is easy to forget that he wrote to the Philippians from the privations of a prison cell.

And how true this is of our Lord Jesus. He had come into our world into a simple, poor family; He had no doubt learnt carpentry helping Joseph, so that the family could eke out a living. In His ministry years He so often slept rough but

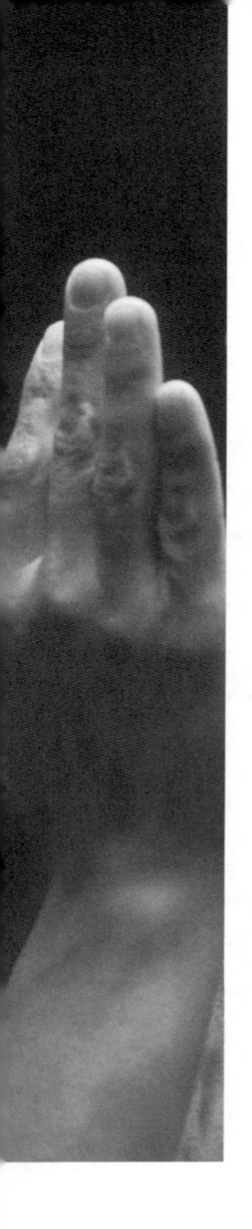

He also appreciated the occasional hospitality of Mary and Martha in Bethany. He had no possessions.

We are bombarded with powerful advertising seeking to persuade us that we *must* have this and that or we *must* take the special offer of a luxury holiday and so on. There is an increasing frenzy for money, profit, gain, with millions persuaded to buy lottery tickets each week as 'it might be you', and the dream that money could buy joy with the big house, the big car, the luxury lifestyle. Yet in rich circles there seems to be little contentment, for there is no lasting joy in things. When you want, want, want it seems you can seldom stop wanting.

But Paul says he has learnt contentment whatever state he is in. Wow!

In writing to Timothy (1 Tim. 6:6–10) he spells it out (read aloud):

> [6]'But godliness with contentment is great gain. [7]For we brought nothing into the world, and we can take nothing out of it. [8]But if we have food and clothing, we will be content with that. [9]People who want to get rich fall into temptation and a trap and into many foolish and harmful desires that plunge men into ruin and destruction. [10]For the love of money is a root of all kinds of evil. Some people, eager for money, have wandered from the faith and pierced themselves with many griefs.'

So it is not evil to have reasonable possessions – what is wrong is the *love* of money.

Contentment in whatever state we are in is not natural. It has to be learnt. The root of contentment has to be that our greatest joy, our greatest comfort, our greatest blessing is all in being Christ's for ever. That is a joy that is not altered by circumstances, as we saw earlier. My diocese of Chester was linked to the Solomon Islands. In establishing the link, Myrtle and I went to visit them in Guadalcanal. One of the most lasting impressions from that memorable visit was their sheer joy in Christ and their simplicity of living. Our respect for coconuts, bananas and fish was greatly heightened!

Many will remember the outstanding Christian leader, John Stott. Towards the end of his life he became very frail; confined mostly to a chair, needing much help and eventually unable to read. He said often, 'I have learned in whatever state I am in to be content'.

The words of verse 13 have been a great inspiration to many followers of Christ, not least me. How can I alter my lifestyle and how can I have control of my money so that I use it for others, not just for myself (this section of the letter arises from the gifts sent by the Philippians, which God would 'credit to their account' – verse 17)? How can I have the strength to make life-choices that the world *may* see as out of step but are in step with Christ?

I can! Yes, I can! Through **Christ** who gives me the strength.

So our focus is again brought back to Christ. The Christ who gave everything for us and who is the **centre** of our lives.

Rejoice in the Lord always. I will say it again: Rejoice!

Discussion Starter

There will be enough to discuss from this section without my asking questions!

Worship

Join in singing or saying Timothy Dudley-Smith's hymn *Lord for the years.*

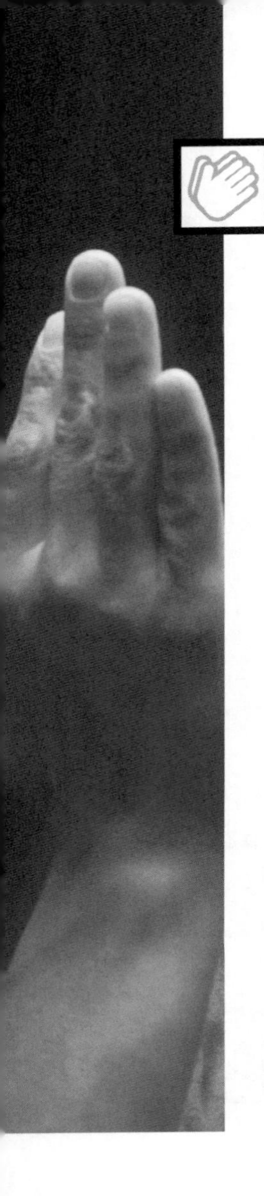

Closing Prayer

First some quiet personal reflection and then, using verses 20 and 23:

To our God and Father be glory for ever and ever. Amen.

As we thank You for Your amazing love for us, we pray that we may live for You, with lives truly centred on Christ.

(And turning to one another:)

The grace of the Lord Jesus Christ be with your spirit. Amen.

Note: We needed to miss verses 8 and 9, where the qualities of goodness recognised in the secular world are Christianised into greater depth resulting in the peace of God with us. It would be a blessing to you if you spent time meditating on them with personal application.

Leader's Notes

Thank you for what you are going to do in leading your group.

I hope you will feel free to handle this material flexibly, perhaps needing to add other questions or to inject other times of quiet or worship.

You will need to make the words of the suggested songs available.

The aim is, of course, to draw everyone closer to Christ but also to be blessed by digging into the Word of God and finding the lasting benefit of getting hold of a whole letter, which will then become a part of the Word in which we feel at home.

It would be appropriate to share a simple Holy Communion after Study Six and/or after some, or all, other sections. The decision is obviously a local one. So is the decision as to whether it is appropriate at any point to have led or open prayer.

Study One

In the opening focus it would be helpful to choose one or more interesting objects to place in sight of everyone; you could even use yourself as a model.

Could you find an old towel that could be cut up into small pieces? Hand a piece to everyone when you get to the first discussion starter.

Study Two

The hymn suggested at the end of this study is powerfully relevant. It is probably best to read rather than sing it, perhaps with the verses read solo by different group members, with everyone joining in the last verse and all of the choruses.

Prior to commencing Study Two, could you kindly formulate the list for the Response section for your own reference. If there is then time to work on this together, you will be able to help the group to work it out. You might like also to point out that when Peter was about to deny Christ, our Lord did not say He would pray that he would not deny Him, but that Peter's faith

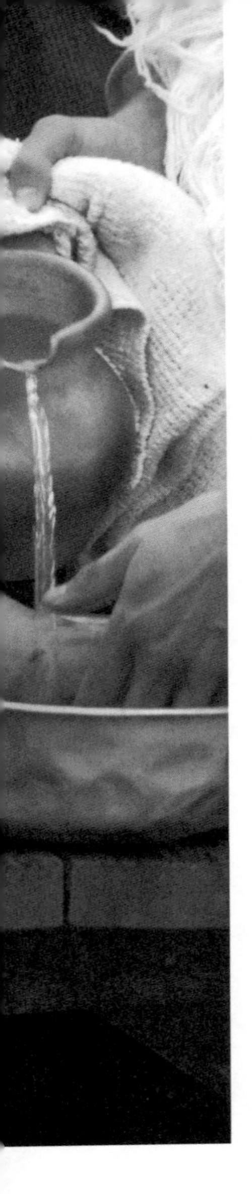

might not fail, and that then, when he had turned back, he should strengthen his brothers (Luke 22:31–32) – Christ's main concern was for spiritual growth.

Study Three

It would be great if you could play a recording of *The Gospel Train* in the opening focus! I have included only two verses of *When I survey* as they are relevant especially to this study, but you may decide to sing it all.

Study Four

If there is time, it would be good to get everyone to look up the three references John 21, Luke 24 and John 11. Together you may think of other incidents like those.

Do you think some form of the Prayer Partnership scheme might work for your group or wider? If so, please open up the idea.

Study Five

In advance of your meeting, would you kindly prepare a list of things to find out about others, eg favourite music, artistic or sporting ability, whether a particular team is supported, where a person was born, whether they are a chocolate-lover, etc? The activity could be done in pairs or by mixing within the complete group.

Study Six

It would be helpful if you could think of a few examples of Discussion Starter 2 after the first section, regarding our Lord's magnanimity (eg the woman taken in adultery).

The mention of worrying (Starter 4) will no doubt touch some lives more than others and sensitive pastoral handling may be necessary during or after the session.

Courses and seminars

Publishing and media

Conference facilities

Transforming lives

CWR's vision is to enable people to experience personal transformation through applying God's Word to their lives and relationships.

Our Bible-based training and resources help people around the world to:

- Grow in their walk with God
- Understand and apply Scripture to their lives
- Equip themselves and their church
- Develop pastoral care and counselling skills
- Train for leadership
- Strengthen relationships, marriage and family life

and much more.

Our insightful writers provide daily Bible-reading notes and other resources for all ages. Our experienced course presenters have gained an international reputation for excellence and effectiveness.

CWR's Training and Conference Centres in Surrey and East Sussex, England, provide distinguished facilities in idyllic settings - ideal for both learning and spiritual refreshment.

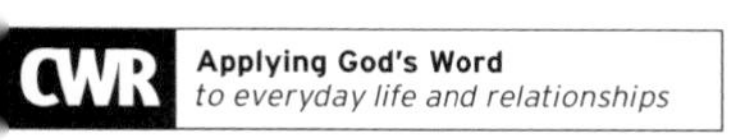

CWR, Waverley Abbey House,
Waverley Lane, Farnham,
Surrey GU9 8EP, UK

Telephone: +44 (0)1252 784700
Email: info@cwr.org.uk
Website: www.cwr.org.uk

Registered Charity No 294387
Company Registration No 1990308

The One Big Question

By Michael Baughen
ISBN: 978-1-85345-792-0

Why does a God of love allow bad things to happen to good people? Michael Baughen's years of biblical study and life experience come together to address this issue and sensitively explore not only the 'why' but the 'how' to deal with suffering. This book will help you come to terms with suffering and will provide some answers to that 'one big question'. This revised edition also contains group study questions.

For current price or to order visit **www.cwr.org.uk/store**
Available online or from Christian bookshops